LEARNING AT HOME

LEARNING AT HOME

AVERY NIGHTINGALE

CONTENTS

CHAPTER 1

Introduction

What can parents and educators do to prevent the decrease of reading motivation during elementary school? The current study provides fodder for thought because the longitudinal decline in reading motivation needs to be addressed by the home, the primary context for fostering the early roots of independent reading habits, before children enter the classroom when reading ability, not motivation, is the focal point of educational debates. A growing body of research suggests that home environments matter a great deal with respect to supporting the development of the kind of cognitive skills necessary to spend leisure time with books. This study is distinctive in providing the first direct analysis of longitudinal trends in the nation's reading levels based on the frequency of parent-child book reading.

National trends in children's ability to read independently have been declining, and lowering reading achievement is having spillover consequences. To improve reading achievement, policymakers, educators, and parents need a fuller understanding of the factors contributing to the decrease in reading motivation. This research provides the first analysis of longitudinal trends in children's independent reading levels using two national data sources. Results suggest that children's reading ability and reading motivation are developing in overlapping but distinct ways. Children have high average reading ability levels in early elementary school but demonstrate strong negative trends over the twelve-year reading development span. However, children maintain or increase reading motivation until around fourth grade, after which motivation to read sharply declines.

CHAPTER 2

Benefits of Learning at Home

S pending time together is a powerful way to help young children feel loved and secure, reducing stress and promoting well-being. Reading to young children reduces stress and encourages bonding between adults and children. Simply talking to children is the most powerful way to encourage language development. Easing stress provides a strong foundation for cognitive development and learning. Research shows that preschool-aged children are stressed when safety and security needs aren't met. Secure attachment between children and adults can lead to positive development in language, cognitive, social, and emotional domains. Educational activities are essential for children. Safe, simple interactions between adults and young children are the best way to promote children's learning.

Learning at home is important for refining skills and promoting awareness of subjects, while allowing children to explore and discover their interests. Children can learn through a variety of activities, regardless of the resources available to them. Here are five learning activities children can do inside the house without going online to supplement learning through formal education provided through their school. Children in primary school and beyond can easily complete these activities with shepherding from their parents or guardians. When introducing these activities, explain how each activity relates to what they are learning at school. Help them to make connections between their day-to-day activities and what they are learning in the classroom.

CHAPTER 3

Creating a Learning Environment

In any room, ceiling hooks are used for hanging student work. Children are given hooks when they are well-behaved, show a special talent, or achieve something new. Those hooks are often used by students as rewards or just as a place to hang up their wonderful pieces of art. Whiteboards, chalkboards, or mirrors on the walls are used to encourage writing or mathematical calculations. This strategy makes learning enjoyable and encourages the kids' other endeavors. All the facilities are delivered on a budget and represents the school at the time. We do not recommend a lot of personal items in school classes, but creating a warm learning environment in the home depends on personalization. Your house is not an art gallery waiting to be photographed. Sure, style is important, but it's not the final goal. This is to create a home environment that cherishes and rewards you and your kids' accomplishments and also it should encourage them to learn and explore the world in an inventive and creative way.

Top-notch facilities are nice, but a learning environment doesn't have to be particularly fancy, says Ron Clark, a top public school teacher and author of the book "The End of Molasses Classes." Clark shares his teaching philosophy and even if he might sound revolutionary, his ideas are quite simple and at the reach of most of us following them. The reading area could be just a space together with our children and read at the same time. A special lamp or string of lights gives a vintage quality to the room. The reading corner is a space that should encourage reading. If you can add comfortable rugs, a rocking chair, or a big cushion, the space will work as a magnet and the room will be filled fast with readers, even with the children that would usually have a hard time sitting still. To encourage writing, give children small notebooks and pens all around; have an inviting place, well lit, using a child's size desk.

CHAPTER 4

Setting Goals and Objectives

Supercharge is the only educational supplement provider to use reported procedures. An expert supercharged kindergarten home learning session, for example, uses Common Core State Standards to identify what would have been taught during academic weeks 32-36. Then the "Kindergarten Supercharged Home Learning Objectives 1-5-23" are carefully crafted to connect to the English language arts, mathematics, and science learning sciences children would have encountered during their 32-36th week at school. Then content objectives are created and reviewed to ensure clear specificity and perfectly align with the KSHLOs. This process can be complex and time-consuming, which may be why many other resource providers bypass it. Unfortunately, being too vague can render educational resources ineffective for learning at home, when students may not have adult "teachers" able to help facilitate learning.

Many home learning resources are "supercharged refresher sessions," picking up right where school instruction left off. Few are backward planned, beginning with identifying the grade-level curriculum standards and objectives that students would have been learning in school at the time, and then writing clear, specific content and teaching objectives that precisely align with those. Insufficiently specific objectives can make learning experiences less effective because they are difficult to monitor and assess. Sometimes traditional lesson planning, which employs backward planning methods, is infeasible for home learning resources because of vague titles and no stated learning objectives or goals. In these cases, the creator normally has to go through the lesson and determine the knowledge and skills students are learning based on the lesson content and then write clear, specific learning objectives to precisely align with those. This can be time-consuming and complex for educators or non-educator creators who were not the original developers of the learning resource.

CHAPTER 5

Selecting Educational Resources

2) , a PTA parent organization, and the non-profit have worked together to provide an online "seal", a web-based designation that vendors use as proof of high-quality educational content. Family members can use the search engine to identify products meeting certain criteria. Examples include an emphasis on content development in areas like math, science, and reading, as well as instructional value, durability, and scalability. publishes a subscription-based trade magazine with expert reviews. Readers paid 900 products for their suitability for schools, home study, and education non-profit organizations. Consumer reports and educational value. Other resources include the monthly publication by the National Association for the Education of Young Children. Educational consulting services can provide hourly rates to work with families in selecting educational content. Open-source online communities can provide both peer and expert support, including Apps with Curriculum and.

1) 5. Selecting Educational Resources: As children spend more time "participating" in technologies that limit their understanding of and interactions with the real world, the importance of parental

guidance increases. For example, swapping blocks with digital puzzles means not interacting with physical objects whose tactile and weight attributes relay information to the senses about the physical world. A variety of resources are available to help parents who are interested in helping to guide children through the digital maze. Resources include which offers ratings on educational content and sites with links for free high-quality educational apps, games, and programs. includes expert reviews and collaborative and interactive learning ratings. The site can help parents discern content that encourages learning aligning with (or conflicting with) educational values important to the family.

CHAPTER 6

Incorporating Technology in Learning

Whether digital media research has the ability to generate above educational tools or methods to some extent remains to be tested. In most cases, research about computers is still in its infancy and digital media has not proved its potential for influencing children's intellectual development. True advancements in reading among young children by older children and functioning are usually not enough for children. According to respondents in recent informal interviews, some preschoolers contribute their technological and digital media advancement to the development. At the same time, however, they worry that the traditional reading of books may be causing them to lose the opportunity to develop their skills in a traditional classroom.

The popularity of the internet goes unquestioned. Many, if not most, children spend significant time online at selected web sites, where they engage in learning activities. These web sites support and enhance children's advanced math and reading skills. Early in elementary school, children have been found to use the internet in an exploratory manner to engage in learning tasks. The truth is that children are often more technologically adept at using the wide variety of digital media available than are their parents or educators. This hype of digital media is apparent even among the very young, and the pace raises all kinds of questions about the impact of technology on learning and child development. Computers are increasingly prevalent in homes, schools, libraries, and are increasingly under scrutiny by public and academic alike. Sales of educational software for children are expected to continue to increase. Nevertheless, the influence of computers is as yet to be fully understood.

CHAPTER 7

Engaging in Hands-on Activities

When a teacher asks, "What did you do in that game?" students have to find the language needed to respond. Games do facilitate conversations and collaborative problem solving that allow teachers to probe and nudge students toward deeper math comprehension. There are also engaging and effective at-home learning tasks - like game play - that invite meaningful conversations, which encourage children to find language and reasoning needed to explain their thinking. To this end, using purposeful games as resources in at-home learning is another great idea that invokes the MATHEdEX's basic principles.

Many museums are now providing virtual tours. Some types of museums that offer virtual tours include history museums, art museums, and science museums. You could also take advantage of virtual tours of world landmarks. What's really cool about this learning idea is that you can visit places that you wouldn't be able to afford to visit in person, at least not until after fans have been rebuilt from the pandemic. The right home-based tasks can take advantage of the learning opportunities that the real world of your home environment provides. As such, consider learning liaisons who engage students in hands-on, family-oriented activities that enhance at-home learning - available via smartphone, tablet, or computer. Moreover, these liaisons have the potential to amplify the teacher's grasp on the nature of the problems students are encountering with at-home, technology-supported learning.

CHAPTER 8

Building a Routine and Schedule

Start and end the day defining the agenda: "At this time you will do this activity", "we agreed that in this period of time you are going to start and from this other limit". Sit with your child to schedule each day of the week. Set times for each activity (not too strict). Although it is also interesting to have moments of flexibility and to divide the week as follows: Monday schedule, Tuesday agility, Wednesday quiet day, Thursday agility. Allow your child to take excursions in formal learning, without pressure. Give them moments of relaxation.

The routines at home, therefore, are going to be the main factor for the construction of discipline, which allows more equitable access to knowledge for all students. The more regular our activities are, the easier it will be for us to build habits and reach them on a more regular basis. It's also easier to measure the progress we're making, the flaws, and to fill in the gaps.

Learning at home when schools are closed should not be left to chance, waiting for inspiration or just happening. Children, like students of any age or even adults, work best when operating in a structured environment within clearly defined schedules. And considering that we are going through an emergency where routine is typically lost, we can help our children regain confidence and emotional safety through these routines and schedules.

Family routines are defined as "predictable patterns of family interaction or habitual patterns of behavior" that serve two purposes: (a) they provide an underlying structure for the family's daily life and (b) they help to coordinate and simplify the daily activities of all family members.

Routines and schedules help us navigate life's uncertain journey and overcome its inevitable chaos. Children thrive on routines and predictability. Routines let children know what they can expect and what the rules and procedures are for everyday events. Long-term scheduling helps children feel more secure because they know what to expect.

CHAPTER 9

Balancing Screen Time and Physical Activities

Live By Example: This is an excellent opportunity to show the children by the example of the parents. Use digital devices with the same eye care as you want for daily use. Show through your own daily behavior that health is integrated into all family activities. Ask your children for help and advice, and provide yours without hesitation in cases where they go beyond healthy limits or find it difficult to fulfill them. Children need to see their parents living and consciously responding to healthy living principles on their own.

Establish a Family Media Plan: This should be a family document that sets the policies for the use of electronic devices at home. Be specific about the places and times that have a restriction (time and place). Outline how to maintain eye health while using digital devices. Outline the activities (education, entertainment, physical exercise) that are important to maintain daily to keep children healthy. Agree to consult the plan periodically to adjust it to new realities and realities.

While it is important for learning, families need to set healthy limits and boundaries on the use of digital screens. This includes setting appropriate limits on television and computer games. The Internet is an indispensable resource for homework and educational activities. However, every child needs consistent and reasonable guidance on the appropriate use of mobile devices for educational purposes. At the same time, educators agree on the importance of maintaining physical activity and exercise. Here are the basic elements to consider in this important problem:

CHAPTER 10

Encouraging Independent Learning

In every subject area, children should receive indirect learning opportunities as well as direct instruction. In the area of language arts, children should be read to and engage in conversations about the text, as well as engage in independent reading and writing. In mathematics, children should receive instruction on the core components of mathematics, as well as indirect learning opportunities that allow children to make sense of the mathematical concepts they are learning or will learn. In the natural and social sciences, children should engage in inquiry and project-based learning in addition to receiving direct instruction on key scientific concepts and critical historical events. For teachers to create independent learners with mastery of content, indirect learning experiences for children are just as important as direct instruction. While it's easier to drill children through direct instruction, creating independent learners leads to deeper conceptual understanding and the development of complex skills. Drill and practice do not lead to an engaged and independent learner. It leads to a child who knows how to pass a test of basic skills but does not know how to think critically, to innovate, or to be a self-starter. Furthermore, when children become independent learners, the classroom teacher is able to be even more effective as a learning guide and practitioner. With a strong foundation of classroom culture and knowledge of the child's individual skills, interests, and concerns, teachers can assign more complex and age-appropriate content to children and engage in more high-level questioning and scaffolding. With this shift, the teacher acts as a learning guide and facilitator as defined by research on good teaching.

When children learn on their own – independently – they question more actively, think more critically, and work harder to be creative and innovative. They process more of what they are learning and debate more actively with their peers. Teachers become more effective because their students are more engaged and curious.

CHAPTER 11

Fostering Creativity and Imagination

Everyone needs to ask questions. Einstein once said that he had no special talent, he was only passionately curious. There is no special talent unique to asking questions, only a passion to feed one's own curiosity. Whenever someone is doing something, you need to ask how they're doing it. If someone takes care of a plant, your curiosity and asking such questions have opened the doors to new things. In a roundabout way, we are all involved in some form of subliminal suggestion therapy. If you see someone caring for the roses, it may not make you actually care for those roses, but if the passion is particularly contagious because of the overwhelming signs of an imminently successful endeavor, it will make you consider what you could be taking care of.

Another pillar that can help shape the future of sustainability is the skill of translating data. If people can visualize raw data in different ways, they can tell stories about what the data means. They can see a trend at a micro-level, and then they can visualize how this trend would function in the macro-world. This combination of visualizing raw data and making this data relatable to the real world impatiently awaits in all of us. We tend to underestimate the power of storytelling, and that's why society continues to get a one-sided view of technology. Let us use the advice of those who came before us. Let us not reinvent the wheel. Let's learn from one another's mistakes and adapt and circulate them into spheres of potential.

Although technology can aid in learning, one of the most important things when people are engaging in their own learning is fostering creativity and imagination. This, of course, starts with storytelling. The act of telling stories, watching movies, reading books, comics, plays, and enjoying activities in miniature are all ways of fostering creativity and imagination. If a person can visualize something, they can make it happen, they can change something, or they can take an idea and make it adaptable—or to use a different word—sustainable. With both adaptability and sustainability in technological development, we want society to take some cues from Nature. The world is full of living things with interchangeable systems and completely sustainable operating systems. Not a single living thing is capable of anything less than sustainability. Embrace this and celebrate it. Make the invisible visible. If we can see it, we can understand it, and together, we can make a better world.

CHAPTER 12

Promoting Social Interaction and Collaboration

Studies have been conducted actively in computer-supported collaborative learning, where technology-mediated learning is supported so that people can learn with others in a possibly computer network, video conference, and collaborative virtual environment. An example is a study by Dillenbourg et al.. They developed the 3Dudnik (a location-based system) for studying social interactions at the university. The system provided a virtual campus that allowed students to use chat (to send text messages) and post notes in discussion forums. They found that physical, not virtual, locations greatly influenced social interactions because students preferred to work in groups with others who would sit close to them. Frequent qualitative observations support these findings explaining why physical distance matters. Social interaction and collaboration in home learning are challenging because of the physical space.

Children can learn with others and also learn from others by sharing ideas, thoughts, and concepts. This is known as social interaction or collaborative learning. Indeed, many cognitive psychologists consider social interaction as a preeminent means of human learning. Students frequently gain motivation and inspiration from others. They also learn by teaching others. They discuss with others, argue about their ideas, and construct understanding through these social interactions. Even every piece of knowledge, initially constructed by individuals, eventually is created through the scaffolding provided by a group. However, this type of social interaction is sometimes hard to acquire in digital environments.

CHAPTER 13

Assessing Progress and Achievement

When selecting from the range of evaluation possibilities, children, parents and educators aware of the wide array of learning styles can consider the variety of formats available: performances, projects, galleries, portfolios, network building, blogging, essay contests, journaling, rap song writing, research investigations, and on-line workshops for women in the sciences, or business, or future time-based travelers—those invention agents like Einstein, or George Washington Carver who illustrate that sticking with a problem, long enough and hard enough, results in great contributions, however invisible in beginning efforts. Public sharing and searching for meaningful feedback in a myriad of community role supports (on-line resources can be critical for family committed instruction) is another potential activity that private schooling can emphasize, and of course searching the world for more and different challenges, from innovators already successful, as well, in two time-zones or more.

Just as removing children from classrooms presents special challenges, deciding how to assess their progress and achievement may be less straightforward than when they are in more familiar contexts.

Drawing upon the atmosphere and procedures used in Finland, where 35% of students fail to graduate from upper secondary school (compared to 80% in the United States), families fearful of direct reference to high stakes tests might consider informal and more continuous monitoring strategies, except where formal assessment is essential to access later course and program options. The agents who facilitate children's progress in the realm of learning can help to support their assessment as well—so, for example, a lack of standardized tests in Finland is made manageable by the strong skills in experiential observation and reflective commentary which teachers are encouraged to diligently develop throughout their university training.

CHAPTER 14

Addressing Challenges and Obstacles

Even constitutional protections or some various national or state-level regulations that protect the right to educate children at home do not guarantee parents the free development and practice of their pedagogical potential, as competitive interests related to universal education come together to create a hostile education and child protection system towards the exercise of this right which constitutes a continuous challenge to the families involved. Families around the world wishing to educate their children have no other choice but to seek refuge in the cracks of the system and the prejudices of many people in order to guarantee their protection and their personal development as a family unit, and ensure the integral education of their children. Regularly, the families involved must influence the perception and acceptance of their right by the rest of the society and the families they defend, making visible to both the plurality and the cultural and educational specificities that are at risk of being homogenized and disjointed under the protective mask of formal education, as well as showing that homeschooling practices can protect the integral development of children, in contexts of vulnerability that often appear, as long as they are not stigmatized and infiltrated by stereotypes and morbid suspicions that end up justifying interference and lack of respect towards education and the development of both children and their parents.

This book has celebrated the tremendous potential of learning at home to enrich and inspire children to pursue an inevitably life-long interest in learning, creativity, and discovery. However, it would be meaningless to deny the presence of enormous challenges in realizing this potential. Many have brought up the indispensable role that formal education has had historically in preserving and advancing human ideals, objectives, and willpower. No learning plan prepared outside formal education can stand against it for long. The traditional education system deservedly commands tremendous respect, while systems and practices of learning entirely outside the school are usually regarded with distrust, if not as corrupt and harmful. One of the greatest obstacles to learning at home is in the form of bureaucratic and institutional resistance from fields related to education. Homeschoolers become some of society's most vulnerable families.

CHAPTER 15

Seeking Support and Guidance

15.2 The Department for Education should ensure that a communication plan includes home education to raise awareness and ensure that parents know where they can be accessed and quality support products that will promote and confirm direct communication with families. Working together with educators from successful schools, academies, and free schools, as well as other experts, assistance during joint communications can be offered. To enable schools, communities, and other organizations in a perfect position to help ensure the spread of appropriate resources, this should also extend to local initiatives.

15.1 Support for parents and young people should be signposted to sources of information on teaching and learning. The Department for Education and the Education and Skills Funding Agency (SFA) should consider working in partnership with other organizations, such as successful schools, academies, and free schools, as well as private sector organizations that provide educational resources. By ensuring that access to these sources of information is made widely available, attendance will be maximized. Time could be saved, and highly recommended sites could be offered by researchers and other experts, including teachers, as part of the Departmental evaluation program and what works in the fields of education.

CHAPTER 16

Maintaining Motivation and Discipline

Expectations around school performance should also be revised to account for increased home responsibilities, feelings of isolation, and a different educational structure – at least that's what students want. "I asked my students to reflect on the first few days of virtual learning," she says. "The most common statement made was that there was much less pressure to succeed. They liked not feeling judged. They appreciated seeing their work grades improve. They understood the importance of interacting with their teachers and classmates and missed the physical aspect of being in school. They liked some subjects, especially the creative and physical education classes, more than the core subjects. They found that there was a lot more work time. And some made a comment that many of us face at home and had home responsibilities."

Set some ground rules and a routine, says New York City seventh-grade teacher Rebecca Cronin. "I ask parents to support their child in creating a school schedule they can stick to with minimal adjustment," she says. "The best way to maintain normalcy is to stick to a regular routine." Offering guidelines can be especially helpful for older students since their school day is structured differently than the in-person or hybrid schedule might be. The same advice applies to teachers too. "In virtual school, everyone needs to be flexible," she says. "But students should be in the habit of getting up and getting ready. They should attend their virtual classes in a quiet place with a fully charged computer and have all the materials they need. They should put silent reading time, lunch or outside time away from a screen on their virtual school schedule regardless of what the other teachers are doing with their time."

CHAPTER 17

Exploring Different Learning Styles

An unsociable student may learn best by quietly sitting by, possibly at a quiet library or carrel, reading and re-reading material. Such a student is an introvert and needs plenty of time alone, especially to think about what they are reading. Note that in general neither of these two students has a learning disability, that they just have different learning styles.

A sociable student may learn best by always working with peers, by asking and receiving help, and by calling and texting friends to discuss the learning material. This type of student should then be free to move in the seat, or walk back and forth, loudly repeating new material and testing each other.

As noted in Chapter 8, most people learn best when they are following their own interests, when they learn at their own pace, in their own ways, using their own preferred learning styles. Every student has dozens of different learning styles, with some, of course, being easier to implement at home than at school. Here are a few of these dozens of learning styles.

CHAPTER 18

Adapting to Individual Needs and Preferences

The personalization model expanded in this research was based loosely on the social interaction approach to language development begun by Vygotsky (1962) and later developed by Andrews (1982), Bain and Vygotsky (1974), Harricker (1982), Haynes (1989), Mindes (1986), and Wertsch (1979, 1985). In Vygotskian terms, each carrier of culture is an individual with a unique learning style, and acquisition of higher level thinking, problem solving, and critical thinking are influenced by the degree of application and effectiveness in verbalizing cultural information, psychological care arrangements, and social interest in participating in the student's learning aspirations. In this research, the human information processing system was also highlighted, and cooperation under the personalized learning model was closely related to communications and helping students surpass constraints in their processing activities received from teachers and parents alike.

Mayer and Harris (1991) found that as schools exert more and more pressure on students to achieve and succeed, a majority of students show less and less desire to participate in activities outside of school (e.g., exploring information through books, reading newspapers, or attending a performance of some type). However, when learning is individualized, much as it is in community-centered institutions such as libraries, museums, and recreational activities, learning preferences, skills, and capabilities direct student behavior into activity participation. Also, a significant finding in this research was that proficiency in individualized learning is made possible by the personalization of human information processing, necessary for both psychological and sociological reasons. In enabling learning modifications identified in this series of studies, a verbal and social interaction approach to learning, teaching, and parenting encompassed problem solving, individual care or guidance on the part of the parents or teachers in dealing with performance problems, and encouragement.

CHAPTER 19

Integrating Real-World Experiences

The instructional design guiding play-4-real tasks follows an if-then-else design, authored to support what Krippendorf calls pragmatic design. This heuristic design or rule-of-thumb approach restricts the number of genuine design roles to be considered, leaving more time for the exploration of meaning, purpose, and insight. The designer should ask if it is possible to perform the skill in that specific context with the same components, as opposed to re-creating the entire engaging activity. Furthermore, the context illustrates the problem-solving role that the skill plays in daily life. By focusing on problems that learners could subsequently solve, the context guides the design of engaging activity, inspires a reason to act, and provides insight by either demonstrating the application of concepts in practice or by providing for the consequences of a poor application of the learner's knowledge. Such a design approach complements instructional theoretical issues and is scalable.

The term "real-world" comes from a particular subset of authentic tasks, namely those that are imitations of the conditions under which the skill would be used in daily life. In many CBT applications, authors are presented with the dual requirements of creating real-world tasks and using genuine contexts, particularly where traditional methods are often demanded by the simulator. Research into the use of these applications has attempted to give guidance on how to accomplish both of these tasks. Real-world CBT (rwCBT) can be defined as being relevant to a particular area of daily life.

Authentic learning involves activities that are real, in a context, and provide knowledge that will be useful instead of knowledge that will eventually be needed. The use of this knowledge is immediate instead of delayed, and it follows the needs of the learner instead of the traditional curriculum. Authentic context is the most complete context for learning. The notion of learning in an authentic context maps onto and extends the notion of situated and constructivist learning. A single educational theory cannot provide the framework for learning in general, but the theory of authentic learning seems to be supported by many educational methodologies.

CHAPTER 20

Encouraging Critical Thinking and Problem-Solving

In every social setting, be it a classroom or a family, the one attribute that a group familiarizes with a good leader is a problem solver or the critical thinker. When I say attribute, I imply that a problem solver will not go unnoticed. The leader might not always be the one who finds a solution to the problem. But the person who finds the appropriate solution for every aspect of the problem will be the leader every time. The quality that most people leave out of the description of a leader is intelligence. It's not about always standing first in class, it is about understanding how and why to use information to make it reach its potential. All the knowledge a person has in the world is of no use unless he knows how and where to apply it to solve problems.

The main point that puzzles me about a superhero's armor or weapon (a gun) combining a beating heart into the design is the possibility it hints towards about critical thinking and problem-solving. In the world of a superhero, there are no two problems which can't be solved by violence or they are never pacifists. But in the real world, we have to look for an appropriate solution to any problem with a lot of thought and care (critically think).

CHAPTER 21

Enhancing Communication and Language Skills

Mrs. Mac and the Melroses (study participants) demonstrated how parent (A-d) metacommunicates with her son (e-h) in response to three-year-old Teddy's repeated assertion that he was angry (e-f). (A) "Mommy I'm getting angry at you" (Teddy), (B) "I was teasing, Teddy" (Mrs. Mac), (C) "Teddy, it's just play" (Mrs. Mac), (D) "I'm teasing Teddy" (Mrs. Mac), (E) "I'm getting really angry" (Teddy), (F) "Teddy, it's just pretend" (Mrs. Mac), (G) "I'm really getting angry at you, Mommy" (Teddy), and (H) "I am still teasing" (Mrs. Mac). Teddy's anger is never understood to exclusively reflect MM's misunderstanding. Instead, Mrs. Mac's (A-d) consistent metacommunication communicates to Teddy that even as his pretend play partner, she hears/understands him throughout their play routines, and she will also remind him that they are engaging in pretend when (F) she repeats her role as MM each communication turns.

Though learning at home is limited to what we do outside of school, opportunities are plentiful! At home, parents can participate in wordplay, which research has continually demonstrated facilitates language and literacy development. Parent-child play is the perfect setting for this playful yet powerful form of interaction. Consider Mrs. Mac and her son, Teddy, as well as the frequent teasing of Teddy's father. To get a good laugh going, Mrs. Mac might 'tease' Teddy by calling him "Sir Teddy," responding "Indeed, Teddy," or replying "The pleasure is mine" when Teddy gives her a card during their game. Later, growing frustrated, Teddy warned, "Mommy, I'm getting angry at you!" Observing her son's escalating feelings, Mrs. Mac immediately apologized, "I'm teasing, Teddy.

CHAPTER 22

Developing Numeracy and Mathematical Abilities

Mothers can support their child's numeracy advancement by promoting math learning deliberately, discovering mathematics styles in daily activities and effectively contributing to an open and interactive math atmosphere at home and in the college. Supporting children to understand and gain confidence in mathematics is another way in which city libraries will enhance children's learning at home. Based on a particular city library program, this method reflects the manner in which a numerically linked activity might be created to reinforce the classroom instruction and improve children's learning. The relationship may not only be quantitatively but also qualitatively effective in school and early experiences that promote powerful methods for working out complex challenges at home or in the classroom. Improve understanding of inter-report relationships and the fact that children's successful mathematical strategies and judgments are a bridge between what they study and what is essential to learn next.

Children learn at a very early age that numbers exist in the world as abstract symbols. You may notice your child pointing to different numerals while they're at the shops, or even starting to identify numbers in their environment. In the Play, Pretend and Do Land activity in this guide, you'll have the opportunity to refine these skills. We are reinforcing mathematically related vocabulary such as 'more', 'bigger' and 'less'; building consistency in 'programming' robots forward and backward; and examining the concepts involved in sorting through the identification of shapes. All important mathematical and numeracy skills are highlighted in the lessons. Children begin to become familiar with such skills as they prepare for the first year in school, such as recognizing and producing simple shapes, sorting, correlating, and setting out objects, and clearly labeling sets of objects (including their own numbers). Numeracy is, for example, an essential part of problem-solving and comprehension.

CHAPTER 23

Exploring Science and the Natural World

Have you ever thrown a rock or a ball? What happened? Compare the rock or ball to a leaf. Use words like around or up to describe your observations. Count how many things you see that are round or shaped like a circle. It goes up and then down. Find some objects in your home and try to figure out how they move by experimenting with them. Sometimes they might roll, sometimes they might slide across surfaces. Shake objects close to your ear and notice if you can hear anything inside. This is an example of how you can use simple concepts of science to explore your home with your child. Ask your child to show you another object or find something that looks like their object. By introducing and using scientific language your child will feel more comfortable using these words.

Exploring science and the natural world. Your environment is your living space and can be described through science. Exploring the world around you can help your child prepare to succeed in school and life. By noticing patterns and similarities between things, children develop an understanding of simple scientific concepts. Animals that fly or birds that swim can affirm your child's understanding of the world. Hands-on experiences with the natural world also help your child to connect language and words with objects in meaningful ways. Consider the following ideas to help initiate discussions about science at home. Engage with everyday materials that introduce science concepts. A leaf or rock can be described using science concepts. Picture puzzles or books for children can be found in thrift stores or a library throughout the year. Find books that allow your child to connect with science at home.

CHAPTER 24

Cultivating Cultural and Global Awareness

We would be woefully remiss to leave out the importance of answering children's questions openly and honestly as part of this process. It's critical for today's young citizens to be as globally aware as they are technologically savvy, so parents need to do what they can to help facilitate that understanding. Parents can fall into the habit of not answering global questions in a way that will promote consideration, or they might answer a question sufficiently without any additional follow-through. This creates a generation of kids who are disconnected and apathetic. We want to build the link between our kids and the newly global world they find themselves a part of. So parents have to respond to as many inquiries as they can, as transparently as they can, in hopes of creating compassionate kids who will lead our increasingly connected world.

Raising culturally aware children involves teaching them to respect and understand those who act, look, think, and believe differently than they do. You can help your children see that (virtually) all kinds of people are part of the greater human family to which we belong. One great way to acquaint kids with other cultures is to read books from stories set in different countries or folk tales from different parts of the world. Additionally, a simple, stress-free way to get started is by including decor in your home that reflects the beauty and richness of various cultures. These items will serve as conversation points or as questions from your children and can also help them show off their awareness of the wider world to friends.

CHAPTER 25

Nurturing Emotional Intelligence and Well-being

The ability to love ourselves, along with skills related to managing emotions and socio-relational relationships, has a fundamental impact on our level of personal well-being and social success. According to the work of Daniel Goleman, who popularized the term emotional intelligence in 1995, together with Peter Salovey and others, personal abilities (motivation and optimism, for example) related to personal well-being are relevant, and are both predicted by academic intelligence. Enhancing the emotional competencies of our family members is the focus of programs for the implementation of social and emotional learning skills (PSE). Nurturing these skills is considered an essential part of education. Emotional intelligence has an effect up to four times greater than intellectual quotients (CI) and competencies during life. The quality of our emotional competencies, social resources, and significant moments and relationships are relevant to increase our vitality and level of happiness.

As parents, many of us will increasingly shift our focus from the quantity of learning to the quality of education that children are receiving. We will also prioritize the well-being of our families. Excessive time spent in front of screens can exacerbate mental exhaustion and lack of sleep. Making time to relax and sitting down to dine as a family can be a valuable tool for improving the overall emotional welfare of our family members. Investing in the care of our emotions and that of others, learning to work as a team, taking ownership of our successes and failures, treasuring the success of others, looking for our own path, improving communication and problem-solving, fostering a culture of effort, and motivating us from adversity are basic aspects in the development of the emotions and relationships of our family members.

CHAPTER 26

Promoting Physical Health and Fitness

Spending time in an interesting and quiet spot with a book and a flashlight or headlamp in the evening, especially during the school year, will help you wind down and relax your mind and body. That is a good thing, because once you get home from school, especially if you are a student in middle school, you may have a list of things to do, such as eat a healthy snack, do your homework, review or study what you learned in class, and, above all, go outside to play, jump, ride bikes or run around to ensure that your body gets exercise and fresh air. You should also make sure to go to sleep at the right time so that you wake up rested the next day, full of energy to continue learning and enjoying life.

What is a comfortable spot for reading and relaxing that you can use when you are at home? What can you do in that spot? Try to use that spot every day. You might want to read about animals, plants, science or other things that interest you. In addition to reading non-fiction, you can also enjoy other things in your comfortable spot, including books based on movies, TV cartoons or comic book characters. Have you ever pretended that you were trying to solve a mystery alongside clever detective Nancy Drew or detectives the Hardy

Boys? Have you ever imagined living in a magical world or being part of a wizarding school, like Harry Potter?

CHAPTER 27

Connecting with Nature and the Outdoors

Connecting with nature at an early age is explained to have deep and long-lasting emotional, intellectual, and spiritual impacts. For one, the outdoors is an engine of curiosity and provides children areas in which they can experiment and observe the world. If the right questions are encouraged, curious children will be conversing with nature rather than passive spectators. This mindset encourages children to foster a critical thinking skillset that will allow them to develop the friendship they need with the world. Furthermore, pay attention to the outdoors and it will teach in a myriad of ways. Unconventionally, nature becomes the child's teacher in a puzzle. It engages all the senses. Just by sight and feel, children learn from the textures of grass, rocks, leaves, and the animals they may encounter. A sniff of a flower, a lick from a puppy dog, the touchdown of a butterfly, or a ray of sunlight on a raindrop creates a world of stimulus. Ultimately, learning outdoors, amidst a virus or in better times, in an outdoor classroom or just in a backyard encourages health and physical fitness through exercise. The natural world provides an arena in which children can learn and experience interactive relationship patterns.

Beyond the classes, books, and essays, what are we really imparting to our children? Acclaimed education and creativity expert, Sir Ken Robinson argues that the social and emotional experiences that define a person's interactions with others are among the most vital of all experiences in education. And in this time of self-isolation, parents may need to reassess exactly how their children are engaging with society. Despite the self-isolation, nature has not been canceled. While school may be online and parks may be closed, there are still many opportunities for children to learn about the natural world and connect with what we have come to know as Mother Earth. Outdoor exploration and fresh air can be the breather that children are in need of. It is no secret that being outside is a powerful avenue for fostering children's growth, play, conservation, and stewardship. Whether it be just looking outside from a hole in the fence, through a window, or actually standing amidst the fresh air with the grass under their feet, children must not forget the warmth and tender love that emanates from nature.

CHAPTER 28

Encouraging Lifelong Learning Habits

One of the forgotten side effects of education is the obligation to help a student develop into a learner. Learning is not about textbooks, lessons, and lectures. Learning is about habits of mind, exposing oneself to the variety of human thought and experience, long after your last routine syllabus. Learning is the ability to figure out the unknown, solve routine challenges in uncommon ways, identify unspoken rules while feeling at home in strange environments. Testing offers some insight, but truly knowing requires the understanding that learning does not end with a certificate, diploma, or even retirement. Since ancient times, pets have functioned thusly, with fortuity providing not only companionship but enduring life lessons for children and adults alike. Recent studies of the human-animal bond even suggest real health benefits with respect to physical activity, personal growth, and reduced incidence of psychiatric conditions such as anxiety and depression. While many articles promote streamlined curriculum in pursuit of higher test scores, and others share the advantages of student attendance at historically popular outdoor adventure programs, the truly compelling issue of learning at home remains.

In many respects, the Long Barracks of the Alamo is a sea of contradictions. As a "must see" destination for tourists and spring breakers, it serves as a microcosm of learning in the modern age. Its foreboding, yet beautifully simple architecture could easily stand as an edifice to the lessons of history, yet its proximity to the South Alamo Park - 800 yards of festively painted arrows, joined by a dotted line, encouraging people to take their next selfie as they walk, step by step, to the famed front door. What should be a place of reverence is instead a living, digital platform that connects us to the past through the jokes and gestures of day-tripping school kids, pre-Instagram thirty-somethings, and Eastern European businessmen. For one red-shirted park ranger, this mix of reverence and irreverence stands as a call to action. His job - to balance tradition and cutting-edge technology wrapped in an understanding that an appreciation of history is not a destination, but a journey. For this ranger, lessons learned at a desk in a fl edged seat bus don't always transfer to streetside knowledge. Neither do sound bites, nor staged interactions. Instead, he understands that true learning demands participation for all the senses, offering the depth and variety of first-hand experience as a key to unlocking the imagination and curiosity of future generations.

CHAPTER 29

Reflecting on Learning Experiences

While students possess varying levels of general abilities and interests in their learning and education improvement, the peculiar experiences at campus such as reunion, general class discussion, presentations of class assignments, and thesis internships offer social learning interactions by engagement, disagreement, or agreement to peers' divergent thinking and course improvement inputs. The weak student learners in the classroom have the capacity to role-play and/or practice student-led teaching discussion sessions or several teachable issues in the related subject outside the classroom. Reflective learning opportunities may also be availed in a formal outreach at the lower academic levels, interaction in informal faculty club, or local gatherings at campus. An academic briefing/orientation to leverage available mentor(s) within the institution should be achieved with graduate students for further reflection if not one-to-one structural meeting of campus learners with their experts.

The practice of "reflective teaching" is unique. Reflections should underpin the "didactical triangle" by ensuring that there is coherence between what the instructor aims to accomplish, his/her strategy association or "didactics," and the available teaching materials or "technology" in the realization. This is an interactive process where learners are given an opportunity to rethink or introspect by asking themselves key questions such as how or what they learn. According to Takanen, reflections are conducted internally or by use of various educational tools such as teacher-learner collaboration, teacher diary, and single and group discussions in the classroom. While an anticipation (premonition) and effort to cover courses (anticipatory) are also important, an in-lesson debriefing, a debriefing session between individuals, groups, and/or instructor and learner(s) are valuable reflection periods that strengthen the reflective teaching practice.

CHAPTER 30

Celebrating Achievements and Milestones

These celebrations can be as simple as a special hug to acknowledge well done or time spent playing or doing an activity they enjoy. Let them know that you are proud and that you admire their dedication and hard work. It's important to also take time to banish self-doubt and fear of failure if things don't always go to plan. Your attitude as a parent to failure helps to shape your child's perspective of it too. Encouraging your child to be adaptive, resilient, and believe in their abilities can take a minor setback and turn it into a success. To do this, remember that failure, setbacks, and mistakes are important components of learning. Allow your child to talk about what they believe they did wrong and help them understand different ways they might approach a similar situation differently in the future.

Your child may not be able to have the typical end-of-year celebration they are used to, with most schools closing indefinitely around the country, nor can they see their friends to share in the delight of their achievements. You can enhance your virtual learning and encourage your child by hosting a celebration. Celebrate your child's hard work and efforts. If they read a new book, complete their lessons, or do well on an assignment or quiz, let them know that they are doing a fantastic job.

CHAPTER 31

Transitioning Back to Classroom Learning

In previous blogs, I have addressed technology and interventions that can help parents and children overcome academic hurdles brought on by the COVID-19 pandemic. Fortunately, the education, nonprofit, and technology sectors have all swiftly responded to help parents who would like to further enrich that learning. The end goal of learning time activities is to engage children and get them to think, act, and reflect on the activities they are doing and the methods and resources that technology provides, such as the activities on Learning Time that test young readers' comprehension as they interact with digital books using a finger or touch stylus. Educators and policymakers have been aware of this issue for months, implementing plans to help students catch up. There is still so much work that needs to be done to protect and enhance the learning process for every child in our country.

A recent article in Education Next highlights that the debate about how and when to transition back to traditional classroom learning has left one critical question unanswered: How will the months of lost learning impact students across the country? That leaves educators and parents on their own, not just to contend with the health concerns around COVID-19, but also crafting solutions to the learning losses their children have experienced. The authors determined students would return to school having forgotten approximately half of what they would have learned had the pandemic not occurred. Here are some resources you can turn to for help.

CHAPTER 32

Conclusion

While many children in sub-Saharan Africa do not receive education in a formal school setting, the learning experiences from those in school are also largely home-based or fall under the broad category of learning at home because of COVID-19. Of the estimated 107 million African children between 5 and 17 affected by school closures, only 9% were engaging in some form of remote learning through radio, television, information and communication technology (ICTs), or some form of distributed materials through printed media or digital devices. The majority of learners, therefore, largely learn without the active interaction of a teacher. Furthermore, studies in Kenya, Ghana, Rwanda, and South Africa show there is often uninspiring transient teacher-student contact, low learning achievement, and overall low literacy and numeracy levels of the majority of the learners upon completing more than six years of basic schooling in sub-Saharan Africa. Learning at home has the potential of contributing to providing the necessary impetus for effective in-school transitions, which require learners to leave the very supportive learning environment of the 'home' to onerous, less supportive, solitary, and rote-based learning environments of schools. Regrettably, the lack of home-school connectivity, therefore, implies that little exists to make this transition seamless but instead, learners get overly burdened and become unable to connect the disparate dots in their short school lives.

The home is a child's first classroom and the first school for most children in Kenya and beyond. African children start learning from the time they are born, with their families and communities, who then hand them over to the teacher to reinforce what they have acquired. In the first five years, a child's mind is more receptive than it will ever be in the rest of life. Parents and families continue to be critically important to children's learning throughout their official school years and beyond. As the African proverb says, "It takes a village to raise a child."